QUIET

PRACTICAL AND EASY STEPS

THE

TO FIND PEACE AND TRANQUILLITY

MIND

WRITTEN BY

GABRIELLA WEEKES

A BEGINNERS' GUIDE TO MEDITATION

Quiet The Mind: Practical And Easy Steps To Find Peace And Tranquillity

First Edition: June 2023

To contact Abanico Publishing, please email: info@gabriellaweekes.com

'Don't feel badly if you find yourself too restless
to meditate deeply. Calmness will come in time,
if you practise regularly. Just never accept
the thought that meditation is not for you.
Remember, calmness is your eternal, true nature.'

— Paramahansa Yogananda

CONTENTS

INTRODUCTION

We live in a time where distraction and entertainment are at an all-time high. With the rise in popularity of social media platforms such as Instagram and TikTok, plus on-demand streaming sites such as Netflix and Amazon Prime, our attention span is slowly (or rapidly) decreasing. At the time of writing this book, on a global scale people are averaging around seven hours of screen time per day (1).

The stresses we experience in our daily lives, especially in big cities like New York and London, can at times make relaxation, and even sleep, a challenge.

Not only do many of us have the fear of missing out (FOMO), we can also find it very hard to switch off, even when we know we want to.

Today we have 24hr instant messaging, voice notes, emails, smart phones and tablets all giving us constant access to communication. We may try to reserve time for ourselves by scheduling a week or two for a holiday once or maybe twice a year. Yet often our days run into weeks and sometimes even months pass before we realise we are caught in an endless cycle of activity and 'busyness'.

Overwork has become a bit of an addiction in Western society. I can think of several people I have worked with in recent years who wore their addicted-to-work tendency as a badge of honour, as if being a workaholic gives you some sort of added value and worth.

I am here to tell you, it doesn't!

And if you've ever experienced burnout, or felt close to it as I have, you will know something has to give.

We are not machines; we need to rest. It is our birthright, not a luxury, to carve out time for self-care.

I have always been someone who values my free time. I am a work-to-live, not a live-to-work person, and getting the balance right between the two is something I put great value on.

However, despite considering myself an advocate of all things mindfulness and meditation, I still fall off my metaphorical meditation cushion more often than I'd care to admit.

The key here is in the verb: we practise meditation. And like riding a bike, it is something we can perfect over time.

There is no right or wrong. It's a completely different experience every single time.

We don't have to judge ourselves. Meditation is unique for each individual. And as the saying goes, all roads lead to Rome, and ultimately it's about finding the route and technique that work for you.

So if you're completely new to meditation, or simply feeling curious, then this guide has entered your life for all the right reasons. There is a plethora of styles and techniques out there to explore, and this book is designed to give you a flavour of some of them, especially those that have worked best for me, because the truth is this stuff really does work!

What if I told you that a simple 5-10 minutes of regular daily practice of meditation could be just the thing to help you to:

- Carve out more free time
- Feel more present and grounded
- Improve concentration
- Increase memory
- Minimise your tendency to react rather than respond
- Temper your emotions
- Reduce stress and anxiety
- Relax the body, mind and spirit
- Find peace and tranquillity

Meditation is on many people's radars these days.

There are apps to follow, and countless international retreats to attend. The Buddha's teachings from 2,500 years ago have spread far and wide. At the time of writing this book, there are somewhere in the region of 275 million people practising meditation all over the world (2), which given our current world population of 8 billion people and counting (3), means there is still a huge opportunity for people to benefit from this ancient spiritual practice.

Where to begin? This is a question I have heard many people ask in my workshops over the years. There are so many styles of meditation to choose from. How do you find the technique that works for you?

This is where I come in!

Over the next five chapters I will take you on a journey of exploration of meditation, giving you the lowdown on a handful of techniques to help get you started.

I spent over nine years exploring different types of meditation techniques and traditions, spending most of 2018 living life not too dissimilar to a Buddhist monk right here in my home town of London. I was meditating for hours every day, abstaining from all worldly pleasures.

I admit I was obsessed with meditation back then, and though I definitely took things to the extreme, through trial and error I have slowly but surely carved out and shaped a practice that works for me.

My aim with Quiet The Mind is to make the practice of meditation a lot more accessible to people. After all, it is a tool that once learned is something you will have for life. What's more, it is completely free and accessible to all.

I will help you to embark on your own meditation journey with motivation, guidance and support based on my years of research and study.

In a nutshell, I have done all the leg work, so you don't have to.

Between 2017 and 2022 I attended many 10-day silent meditation retreats, trained as a yoga and meditation teacher in India, was initiated into Beeja Meditation here in London, qualified in Yoga Nidra also in India, before eventually plucking up the courage to start sharing guided meditations online.

These are available on YouTube, via live sessions, and via recordings on my very own teacher page on the Insight Timer app (I have included links to these in the last chapter of the book).

I also featured in a national newspaper in the UK, *The Daily Telegraph*, sharing insights on my personal meditation journey, and was invited to write columns on mindfulness in two national magazines.

More recently I have linked my love of dance and meditation by creating a movement meditation practice that I share at regular in-person workshops in London, and have found them to be a powerful and rewarding technique for myself and others.

The truth is, however, that as I continue to evolve through life, my meditation practice changes too. What really works for one period of time eventually opens up new doorways of exploration. And even if we forget for a while, we always have infinite opportunities to begin our practice all over again.

In gratitude,

Gabriella

CHAPTER ONE

Meditation, The Basics

The Collins English Dictionary defines meditation as 'the act of remaining in a silent and calm state for a period of time, as part of a religious training, or so that you are more able to deal with the problems of everyday life'. (4)

As the Buddha stated over 2,500 years ago, life is suffering. We are inevitably going to have challenging experiences in our 75-odd years in this game called life, and that's if we're lucky. Whether it be physical, psychological or relational, we all have our obstacles to overcome, lessons to learn, and growth to experience. I like to think of life as a kind of soul school.

What the Buddha also found through his own exploration was that there is a way out of suffering, and that way is through the practice of meditation. He realised that both our grasping for pleasure and our aversion to pain are ultimately futile, because everything either ends or changes form. Change is the only real constant.

And I know how hard it is to accept that approach when you are in the midst of despair, or grief at the passing of a loved one, or facing the reality of falling ill with a life-threatening disease, or finding your partner has run off with someone else. These things can take a huge toll.

However, the truth is, if you're here reading this book, then like myself you have survived every single experience you have gone through up to this point. You are so much more powerful, capable and blessed than you can ever know.

Mind Management

When I first started meditating, in 2014, it felt really difficult to commit to anything for more than a few minutes, without the guidance of a teacher. I remember reading a book on mindfulness which had a series of short daily exercises to practise over a period of several weeks, to help track your progress.

I also recall being introduced to one of the more well-known meditation apps at the time, and exploring some guided meditation recordings for a while, although I never really warmed to the teacher's voice.

Like any new habit, we need to start with baby steps, and slowly work our way up to longer periods of time. So don't get disheartened if you think you are not doing it correctly to begin with.

The mind has a sneaky way of wriggling out of meditation — you'd be surprised at how creative it gets at inventing excuses and reasons why you are unable to meditate for 1, 2, 3, 4 or 5 minutes at a time. There is an oft-repeated quote in a book by Robin Sharma, which is: 'The mind is a wonderful servant but a terrible master.'(5)

I often like to compare the mind to a wild horse.

Now, if we're not careful, a wild horse can be pretty dangerous. But through training, we can begin to build a harmonious relationship with it.

Our mind can be unruly and judgmental. It sometimes feels as if its sole purpose is to prevent us from stepping outside our comfort zone, or from seeking growth or personal development.

The ego mind is all about safety, for it has managed to keep us alive this long, so when we discover a tool that can actually dampen its power over us, it takes that rather personally.

Environment

The environment, or location where you choose to meditate will have a massive impact on your overall experience. I have found that choosing a consistent location where I repeatedly go to meditate is hugely beneficial in establishing a regular routine.

You are programming the mind to recognise this particular location as your 'meditation space', which will help you drop into the right vibe every time.

If space is limited for you, then a simple area of floor space in your bedroom or living room works really well.

Avoid practising in bed unless you are specifically practising meditation for sleep, such as Yoga Nidra for example, as our mind already associates our bed with sleep. What begins well can often lead to slumberville, and hey, that's not always a bad thing, especially if you habitually struggle to settle.

Posture

Whether sitting on a chair, on the floor in lotus pose, or lying down, posture is key. It's important to maintain a straight spine throughout your practice where possible.

It's not good to be tense in your posture, as that also tends to detract from relaxation. Many people think they're only doing a practice for the mind, although I have found that prolonged meditation can relieve the body of everything from muscle tension to skin conditions.

If you have physical limitations, then find a seat or chair that works for you.

When on retreat, I tend to build a bit of a meditation fortress out of cushions and blankets. The more comfortable the better for me. When at home I tend to keep it really simple by sitting on the floor on a sheepskin rug.

I tend to lose circulation in my feet after a long period of time sitting cross-legged or in lotus pose, so I do have to wriggle into new leg positions while seated. Ultimately your body will have its own quirks, so work with what you've got. Sometimes a soft chair can do wonders, other times laying down on a yoga mat. Whatever floats your boat.

In terms of posture what is key is to keep the back nice and straight so your head and neck are in line with the spine, and you're not slouched (where possible). If you are not sure what to do with your hands, you can place them on your lap or on your knees. Palms can face up or down.

Clothing

It may seem obvious, but what you wear to meditate can require a bit of thought. Generally I would avoid these items:

- Jeans — even baggy denim can feel a little stiff in certain areas, and if you're sitting down to meditate there is a high chance it will start cutting off the circulation in those tight areas.

- Tight underwear — anything tight and restrictive will annoy you after a period of time.

- Knitted wool items — not only will this likely get too hot, but some woollen garments can be particularly itchy, so best avoid unless you are not sensitive to coarse textures.

- If meditating in a group session, avoid tight or revealing clothing so as not to distract other meditators. In more traditional group meditation sessions or on retreat, both men and women wear sarongs.

When To Practise

For me what works best is top and tailing my meditation practice at the beginning and end of each day. I find that practising first thing is an excellent time to meditate. First, because it feels as if the rest of the world is still asleep, and second, because upon waking we're pretty much already in the same brainwave frequency as in deep meditation, so it can segue quite nicely.

And meditating just before bed is a great way of switching off from my day, winding down and setting myself up for a good night's sleep.

I try and keep to the same length of time for both my morning and evening sessions. Currently I meditate for 11 minutes per session (morning and night). I think anywhere between 5-20 minutes for a standalone session is both achievable and beneficial while navigating busy city life.

I used to meditate for hours a day, and honestly it didn't leave much time for anything else. If you're on retreat, you can expect to meditate anywhere between 5-12 hours per day. And this is only really possible because you have a team of people managing the schedule and your food preparation throughout.

The truth is, everyday life, especially in the West, is not conducive to lengthy meditation sessions, although in the beginning it's probably natural to get slightly obsessed by it, especially after you start noticing the benefits.

And sometimes twice a day is just not going to work. We all have people who depend on us, or commitments to work, our partner, family and friends. Meditation should not detract from any of that. If anything, meditation will actually begin to slow time down, giving you more of it to share with the people and the projects you love the most.

The Breath

Our breath is by far the most important part of our meditation journey. Connecting to the breath can quite literally change your life.

A lot of what we deem to be 'anxiety' can actually be remedied by regulating our breathing patterns. A dysfunctional breathing pattern links to our nervous system. Often we can be walking around in levels of serious flight or fight, or freeze response and have no idea. By bringing awareness to our breath through our focused attention, we can start to control our breath patterns to bring a sense of calm and tranquillity to our body, and following that our mind.

The breath is the foundation of all meditation. It's a great starting point, and honestly provides instant results. On many of the 10-day silent retreats I have attended, the first five days are simply focused on the breath, before even beginning the meditation technique. That's how key our breath is for successful meditation.

Looking out in the world of wellness, there is an abundance of breathing techniques to choose from. Everything from pranayama, holotropic, shamanic, Wim Hof, etc. Some techniques are designed to energise and activate, such as kundalini yoga, while others are better suited to relaxation, such as alternate nostril breathing.

During my yoga teacher training in India in 2019, I learnt that our body's energy and breathing patterns are in a constant state of flux. So expecting any form of yoga, or meditation practice, to be exactly the same every time is not realistic, and that is actually quite liberating. These practices are about your individual experience in the moment, so even if you're sharing the practice in a group, there is no need to compare.

I tend to be quite an energetic person, so I naturally gravitate towards the techniques that help to soothe my nervous system, calm the mind, and help to deepen relaxation. And if you are reading this book I would make a guess that this is what most of you are looking for too. The good news is that all of it is available to you, and you can always dip your toe into one technique to see how you get on, let it go, and move on to something else. Curiosity and an open mind are key.

What's great is that as we're basically breathing all of the time, we can call on these techniques whenever we need, no matter our location or environment. I often practise breathing on my daily commute, when I am at work, after a long day, in the bath, at the gym.

In a nutshell, the more you inhale using your nose, and the more you elongate your exhalation, the calmer your nervous system becomes. This is science!

Given the increased diagnosis today of conditions such as ADHD, depression, stress and anxiety, mastering your breathing can massively boost your emotional and mental health and wellbeing.

Whenever I am particularly stressed I sometimes find it negatively impacting on my sleep. I can wake up in the middle of the night, sometimes in a panic. With practice I have learnt that by simply slowing down my breath, lengthening my exhalation over a series of, say, 10 breaths, I immediately start to feel my heart rate begin to slow, which sends a signal to the brain that all is well, and there is nothing to fear.

Here are a selection of simple techniques to get you started.

Start by setting a timer for five minutes once a day for a period of seven days, and give one of these techniques a try.

When you have completed all seven days you can move on to another technique for another seven days, and so on. Before you know it 28 days will have passed and you will have sampled four different breathing techniques, giving you some insight as to which one worked best for you.

Then you can always try to incorporate your favourite technique into a daily routine, perhaps in the morning upon rising, or at the end of the day before bed:

- **Nostril Breathing** — While in a seated comfortable position either on a cushion or chair, with eyes remaining closed, bring your focus of attention to your nostrils. Begin to notice the air travelling in through your nose as you inhale, and out of your nose as you exhale. What do you notice about the air on the inhalation compared with the air leaving on the exhalation? Can you sense or feel the tip of your nose? The aim is to focus on the sensations in your nostrils. When thoughts come, simply bring your attention back to your breath.

- **Box Breathing** — This technique is all about bringing regularity back to our breath. While in a seated, comfortable position, bring your focus of attention to your breath. Begin to inhale for a count of 4, hold for a count of 4, and exhale for a count of 4. Repeat this for a set length of time. What did you notice about this technique? How did you feel after the practice?

- **Alternate Nostril Breathing** — You need your right hand for this. Adopt a comfortable seated position with a straight spine. Inhale through the left nostril for the count of 4, while pressing the right nostril closed with your right thumb. Hold both nostrils closed for a count of 6, and exhale through the right nostril for a count of 8, while pressing the left nostril closed with your right index finger. Inhale through the right nostril for 4, hold for a count of 6 and exhale from the left nostril for a count of 8, alternating pressure on the opposite nostril every time you inhale or exhale. If you want to try different counts of breath and holds please do so, as holding for 6 can be quite challenging for some at first, likewise exhaling for 8. Take this at your own pace. Was there a difference between nostrils when alternating the breath either side? Was one side more blocked than the other?

- **Calm The F*@k Out Breath** — In either a seated or prone position, using nasal breathing only, inhale for a count of 4 and exhale for a count of 8, repeating continuously. What do you notice during this breath? Has anything changed since practising this?

It would be amazing if we could learn this stuff in school, setting up children with these useful tools for life. However, whether you're in your early 40s or late 60s and are completely new to all this, there is no better time to start than the present.

Top Tips

- **Release all expectations** — Just because one technique works for one person, it doesn't necessarily mean it will work for you. There is a whole smorgasbord of meditation techniques for you to try from chocolate eating to candle gazing.

- **Start small** — You only need to allocate small chunks of time to familiarise yourself with the basics, and once those become second nature, you can move on from there, increasing the time for your practice, and eventually exploring completely new techniques.

- **Let go of judgement** — The key here is to be kind to yourself. As with learning any new habit or skill, there will be some initial hurdles to overcome on your way to mastery. Your inner critic and saboteur will throw every excuse at you, from 'I am too tired', via 'I'm too busy' to 'I need to check my social media'. There will always be excuses to hand. By practising today, you are making a commitment to your future self.

- **Delay gratification** — Doing something in the short term which will have long-term benefits can be a powerful tool for delaying gratification and seeing things through to the end.

Now that you have all the basics, I think you're ready to start diving into some specific techniques. Mainly the ones that have proved the most beneficial to me on my own meditation journey.

You are more than welcome to skip ahead to different sections if you so wish. However, I have deliberately listed these in the order in which I recommend you explore them, starting with the simpler grounding techniques, through to the more advanced meditation practices.

CHAPTER TWO

Grounding

Right now, in 2023, the western world is going through a mental health crisis which seems to be getting more severe year on year.

While technology has provided us the means to stay connected with people all over the world, at any time of day, we have never felt more disconnected and isolated than at this time.

Let the statistics speak for themselves: 'The number of anti-depressant items prescribed over the past six years has increased by 34.8 per cent, from 61.9 million items in 2015-16 to 83.4 million items in 2021-22.' (6)

People are relying on a quick fix of medication to sort out a lifetime of stress and upset nervous systems that come from living in mass populated cities. Every single day we are bombarded with noise, pollution, media and advertising as well as electric and magnetic fields (EMFs).

Our systems our often over-stimulated and yet we believe a pill can fix us. The reality is that medication, while certainly helping people to feel better in the short term, doesn't look at root causes, and only treats the symptoms of the problem.

I do, however, believe there is a solution which is a lot simpler than we realise.

It was through navigating my own challenges with mental health which helped me see that a lot of what I went through was caused by what is more widely known as being ungrounded. To be ungrounded is to be disconnected from our body. And believe me, we can still technically operate as a human being when we're ungrounded, though it's as if everything seems really intense, chaotic, fast, emotional, irrational and reactive.

This is usually a clue for me, when things start to turn slightly weird, or I feel as if time is literally speeding up and I have to rush everywhere.

Perhaps you have experienced the same, or maybe not. I can only share from my own personal experience.

For me it's a bit like being stuck in some alternate reality where one moment I have 10 minutes to leave the house for work, but the next, after brushing my teeth for no more than a minute or so, I only have one minute left to catch my train. This is usually my clue; perhaps you will find ones of your own.

Usually when this happens I feel super-angry and frustrated because of the knock-on effect of time slipping away from me. If I can catch myself, I will start to use some of the tools I have to slow things down again, such as the breath, as described in the previous chapter, but also through visualisation.

The simplest way to ground is by going out into nature, taking your shoes off, and placing your feet on the earth for about 10 minutes. This helps to transform all the positive ions to negative ions in the body. If you think of the earth as having a frequency, we have a frequency too, and if we spend a lot of time surrounded by technology our frequency starts to shift. By coming back to nature we can re-attune ourselves to our natural frequency, which is the negative ions that the earth emits.

I appreciate the above is probably more of a seasonal activity. I'm not really keen on walking barefoot on open ground during winter, it's more like a muddy/frosty swamp out there from November to February, and this is when visualisation can really help provide you with the benefits of grounding when real nature is not an option for you.

Grounding for me is all about bringing my energy down from my head towards my feet, and even down into the floor beneath me. There are a number of visualisations you can try, but I will share two with you.

I recommend you try this every day for 14 days. The longer you ground the better. I would start anywhere between 5-10 minutes. Try it in the morning to set you up for your day.

Liquid Honey (Recommend 2-5 minutes)

This meditation works well if you are limited for time.

Start by sitting In a comfortable seated position with a straight spine, closing your eyes and becoming aware of your breathing, bringing your focus of attention to your head.

I would like you to imagine that liquid gold/ honey is starting to drip from inside the centre of your head as if you are beginning to pour it from a glass at the centre of your brain.

You can choose to visualise the liquid as more of a waterfall, starting as a trickle and eventually pouring down, in the way you see red lava travel down a volcano.

What I love about this meditation is that your thoughts seem to melt away as the golden light/ liquid pours from your head down your neck and body to the earth below you.

As with all meditations, you can incorporate some breathing exercises to help guide the liquid or simply to help soften and relax into the visualisation.

Sometimes we have to get into the right space for visualisation so it really helps if you include a short breathing exercise before starting the practice.

Rooting Down (Recommend 10 minutes)

The Rooting Down meditation can be practised standing, seated or lying down. Personally, I prefer seated as I can better visualise the earth energy travelling up my spine, although it can be great preparation before bed to lie down.

With eyes closed, take three big breaths in through the nose and out through the mouth.

Imagine you have a giant tap root travelling down from your sitting bones or the soles of your feet, depending on your starting position. These tap roots are designed to drink in energy as if it were water.

In the visualisation you should witness these roots travelling down through the floor below you, and into the earth beneath.

Depending where you are in the world, you may want to visualise travelling down through the concrete floor, then the soil, rock, stone, water and lava and eventually down to the crystal core of the earth.

Once you reach the centre you can either decide to wrap your roots around the core, or simply imagine the roots locking in place.

Once connected, using your breath, you should visualise that warm amber light from the earth travelling up from the core, through your root and into your body.

You should picture this warm energy travelling up the spine, rather like the way steam rises from a kettle. You can either inhale it all in one go, or gradually draw that energy up with each breath as you would drink from a straw.

I also recommend you allow any excess energy to pass through the top of your head; it's surprising how often there will be an outpouring of energy when I practise this.

Give it a try, set the intention, and notice what happens.

The Seven Chakras of the Body

This can be a great chance to work with the chakras of the body as you essentially breathe the earth energy up through the floor beneath you, up through your feet/ sitting bones to the base of the spine and up the spine until it reaches the top of your head.

What you do differently here is imagine the earth energy is clearing and brightening each of the chakras of the body. You can picture it removing any cloudiness, dullness or full-on blockages if that's what you perceive.

Each of the seven chakras (energy centres) of the body represent a different part of our developmental stage in life. Many yogis believe that blockages in these chakras can lead to imbalances in our everyday life. We can work to clear and strengthen our chakras by ourselves to help bring them back into balance.

- **Root Chakra (colour red)** — Starting at the base of the spine. The root chakra is home to our survival instincts, our sense of safety, stability, abundance, health and our sense of belonging.

- **Sacral Chakra (colour orange)** — Located between the sexual organs and below the belly button. The sacral chakra rules all things connected with our sexuality, emotions, relationships, intimacy, sensual pleasure and creativity.

- **Solar Plexus Chakra (colour yellow)** — Located just above the belly button. The solar plexus is all about our willpower, confidence and the ability to act on our goals and bring plans to reality.

- **Heart Chakra (colour green)** — Located at the centre of the chest at the sternum. The heart chakra is the centre of unconditional love both for self and others, compassion, empathy, inner peace.

- **Throat Chakra (colour light blue)** — Located at the centre of the neck. The throat chakra is all about communication, how we express ourselves and speak our truth.

- **Third Eye Chakra (colour indigo)** — Located above the eyes in the centre of the forehead. The third eye chakra rules our intuition, psychic ability, inspiration, wisdom, perception and sight.

- **Crown Chakra (colour purple)** — Located at the top of the head. The crown chakra rules all things connected with faith, oneness, enlightenment, awareness, spiritual wisdom and clarity of thought.

When any of these chakras become blocked, or overactive, it could be a sign that there is an area of life that needs your attention, care and love. By using visualisation tools, such as a regular rooting-down meditation practice, we can do wonders for our energetic system as a whole.

CHAPTER THREE

Body Scan

Body Scan (15 minutes to 1 hour)

One of my favourite techniques and one of the reasons I specialised in teaching Yoga Nidra. Of all the meditation techniques I have tried over the years, I have found body-scan techniques such as Vipassana, and especially Yoga Nidra, to be the most effective.

Yoga Nidra can be translated as yogic sleep. One hour's practise of deep Yoga Nidra is the equivalent of four hours' sleep, making it a great practice to develop if you suffer from, or have a tendency towards, insomnia or stress-related issues.

Regardless, we can all benefit from a little more sleep from time to time, and I personally find this to be an awesome practice right before bed.

Why not start with a smaller 15-minute period and slowly build up to an hour. You can choose to come out of meditation at the end by sitting up and closing in prayer, or you can allow yourself to drift off into sleep straight afterwards.

This incorporates both the techniques from the earlier chapters: breath and visualisation play a huge part in body-scan meditation. I recommend practising both breath and visualisation meditation for a number of weeks before you dive into longer-form meditations. This will help you develop your concentration through shorter meditations and build up to longer sessions over time.

This practice is best performed lying down. You may choose to meditate on a mat and under a blanket, as your temperature can drop during meditation, or on your bed. For the latter, however, it is important to set your intention to remain completely awake and aware for the duration of the practice. You will be surprised how many people fall asleep during Yoga Nidra, but if you want to get the most benefit from it the key is to remain in a wakeful sleep state.

Yoga Nidra is best practised away from bright light to avoid distraction. If you have an eye mask I recommend using that. Not only does it help to block out any light, it will help you to draw your focus inside the body.

In terms of posture you should lie in the Savasana yoga pose (the one that you do at the end of each yoga class), on your back, with arms either side of the body, palms facing up and legs spread either side, with your feet turned out. The key is for none of your limbs to be touching each other in order to limit your sensations of touch.

With Yoga Nidra the trick is to start slowing down the use of some of the five senses, which works to heighten our awareness of other senses such as touch and hearing. The aim is to switch off the critical thinking mind and allow the parasympathetic nervous system to come alive, which is the state of rest and digest.

When we are thinking we are in a state of high alert. For example, we can be focused on one thing, or simply talking with a friend, but our senses are constantly alerting us to external events. By giving the mind something to focus on, such as a body scan, we essentially distract it from doing its main job, which in turn helps to promote relaxation.

If we are in a state of high alert for long periods of time, it can lead to sleep problems and eventually ill-health. This is because when our nervous system is too activated, it denies us the opportunity to rest. Yoga Nidra is amazingly helpful with this.

So let's get started.

Yoga Nidra Guided Meditation

Lying down in a comfortable position, with palms facing up and eyes closed, I would first like you to focus on your breath. Inhale with a count of 4 through the nose, and exhale with a count of 8 through the nose.

Now bring your focus of attention to your Third Eye Chakra, which is located in the centre of your forehead directly between your eyebrows. I would now like you to chant the mantra OM silently to yourself for about a minute or so… OM… OM… OM.

Then bring your attention to the room you're in. Become aware of any sounds in the room. Become aware of the surface that you are lying on, and how your body feels in contact with the surface. Feel the weight of your body on the surface beneath you. Notice any initial sensations in your body. Any heat or vibrations, tingles or pain. There is no right or wrong here, simply bring your awareness there. No need to judge.

Now bring your focus of attention to the space outside the room. Become aware of any sounds outside the room.

Now extend your focus of attention far off into the distance. Become aware of any sounds as far away as you can hear. Maybe you can hear a car, or a plane?

Now return to your body, becoming aware of the sensations in your body. Notice any areas of tension and breathe into those areas, imagining healing golden light travelling to those places as you inhale, and that golden light leaving those areas as you exhale. Continue that breath for a minute or so, creating a circuit of golden light.

Before we begin the body scan you now have an opportunity to work with an affirmation. Something that you can recite silently to yourself three times. This is what we call a *sankalpa* and is something that you can repeat every time you practise Yoga Nidra.

An example of a *sankalpa* could be: I am happy, I am healthy, I am wealthy, I am wise.

Once you have completed reciting your *sankalpa,* bring your attention to your right hand. I would like you to imagine, sense or feel your right hand. You don't need to touch any body parts, just imagine or sense them as we work our way around the body.

It is important that you remain completely still and relaxed, while setting the intention to remain awake throughout the practice.

Become aware of the palm of the right hand.

Become aware of the back of the right hand.

Right wrist.

Right forearm.

Right elbow.

Right upper arm.

Armpit.

Right shoulder

The whole right arm. The whole right arm. The whole right arm becoming aware and relaxed.

Now bring your focus of attention to your left hand.

Become aware of the palm of the left hand.

Become aware of the back of the left hand.

Left wrist.

Left forearm.

Left elbow.

Left upper arm.

Armpit.

Left shoulder

The whole left arm. The whole left arm. The whole left arm becoming aware and relaxed.

Now become aware of your right thigh.

Right knee.

Right shin.

Right calf muscle.

Right ankle.

Right heel.

Top of the right foot.

Sole of the right foot.

The whole foot.

The whole right leg.

The whole right leg.

The whole right leg becoming aware and relaxed.

Left thigh.

Left knee.

Left shin.

Left calf muscle.

Left ankle.

Left heel.

Top of the left foot.

Sole of the left foot.

The whole foot.

The whole left leg.

The whole left leg.

The whole left leg becoming aware and relaxed.

Top of the head.

Back of the head.

Back of the neck.

Right shoulder blade.

Left shoulder blade.

Upper back.

Mid back.

Lower back.

Spinal cord.

The whole back.

Right glute muscle.

Left glute muscle.

Back of the right thigh.

Back of the left thigh.

Back of the right knee.

Back of the left knee.

Right calf muscle.

Left calf muscle.

Back of the right ankle.

Back of the left ankle.

Right heel.

Left heel.

The whole underside of the body.

The whole underside.

The whole underside becoming aware and relaxed.

Top of the head.

Forehead.

Right temple.

Left temple.

Right ear.

Left ear.

Right cheek.

Left cheek.

Right eyebrow.

Left eyebrow.

Right eyeball.

Left eyeball.

Bridge of the nose.

Right nostril.

Left nostril.

Top lip.

Bottom lip.

Tongue.

Back of the throat.

Right side of jaw.

Left side of jaw.

Chin.

The whole face.

The whole face.

The whole face becoming completely aware and relaxed.

Front of the neck.

Right collarbone.

Left collarbone.

Right side of the chest.

Left side of the chest.

Right ribcage.

Left ribcage.

Torso.

Abdomen.

Right hip.

Left hip.

Pelvis.

Right thigh.

Left thigh.

Right knee.

Left knee.

Right shin.

Left shin.

Front of the right ankle.

Front of the left ankle.

Top of the right foot.

Top of the left foot.

The whole front of the body.

The whole front.

The whole front becoming completely aware and relaxed.

The whole body.

The whole body.

The whole body becoming aware and relaxed.

I would now like you to imagine your body is becoming heavy.
You feel the weight of gravity, allowing your body to sink deep
down into the earth beneath you. Allow the weight of your bones

and muscles to relax fully into the surface you are lying on. Allow this sense of heaviness to affect your whole body.

I would now like you to imagine your body is becoming light. Imagine your body is becoming as light as a feather. Feel as if you could literally float away. Allow this sense of lightness to affect your whole body.

I would now like to remind you of the *sankalpa* you recited earlier. I invite you to recite this same mantra silently to yourself three times.

We are going to do a quick breathing exercise together. Count down your breath from 21 to zero. If you lose count along the way, you can simply start from the beginning again. If you finish before my count, you can start from the beginning again. Inhale through the nose. Exhale through the nose. Inhale while saying 21 (to yourself). Exhale while saying 21.

Inhale 20. Exhale 20. And so on . . .

Once you have completed the exercise at zero I would like you to visualise a series of objects in your mind's eye. Don't worry if you cannot visualise the images specifically, simply bring the object into your mind's eye, either from your memory or something you have made up.

Mountain.

River.

Ocean.

Sky.

Sunset.

Boat.

Shell.

Crystal.

Palm tree.

Turtle.

Frog.

Rain.

Diamond.

Candle.

Flower.

Painting.

Releasing the visualisation, bring your focus of attention back to your body. With eyes remaining closed, become aware of any sensations in your body.

Now bring your attention back to the room you are in. Become aware of the floor beneath you, and the space above you. Become aware of any sounds in the room.

Now bring your focus of attention to the space outside the room. Become aware of any sounds outside the room.

Now extend your focus of attention far into the distance. Become aware of any sounds as far into the distance as you can hear.

Return to the body, with the eyes remaining closed, bring your focus of attention back to your breath. Inhale for a count of 4, exhale for a count of 8.

If practising this session with sleep in mind, you may choose to stop the practice here and settle in bed.

If you have decided to end the practice, you may start to move your fingers and toes, before turning over on your side and lying there for a few moments.

With eyes closed, you may come up to a seated position and bring your palms together at heart centre.

Together we are going to close the practice with one OM Shanti Shanti Shanti.

Inhale to begin.

OM . . . Shanti . . . Shanti . . . Shanti.

Namaste.

You may now open your eyes and return to the room. Take your time to come back after a long Yoga Nidra session. Be sure to allow yourself enough time to wake up fully before you think about driving or using machinery.

Yoga Nidra is something that deepens with time. I have gone through phases of practising it regularly, and phases where I don't practise it at all, although I always love sharing and teaching this beautiful technique as for me it is very easy to pick up, no matter how little experience you have of meditation.

CHAPTER FOUR

Movement Meditation

Movement Meditation (20 minutes to 2 hours)

Dance and movement have always been a passion of mine. I remember doing ballet as a kid, and going to my first nightclub on holiday in Ibiza with my dad at age 14. I remember sneaking into illegal garage raves in London when I was 17, and many years later training as a competitive samba dancer in 2014, before embarking on a two-year partying journey from 2015. The ultimate dance highlight for me was dancing samba on the streets of the Rio Carnival in 2018, which was a real bucket-list tick moment.

Dance was something that felt good 100 per cent of the time. And scientific studies have shown it is very good for our health too, especially when compared to other forms of exercise such as walking, yoga and cycling (7 & 8).

What I realised during the pandemic, when all the retreat centres were shut, and socialising was off limits, was that I needed meditation more than ever, but because of the incredible stress I was under I couldn't bring myself to sit on the mat.

And that when I needed meditation the most I couldn't do it, because my nervous system was way too agitated and negative thoughts were spiralling out of control.

I realised that I had to find another way that incorporated the body too. And while body scans can most definitely help, it can still be tricky if you have an over-active nervous system, or you are experiencing trauma because your body is literally in a state of fight or flight, which is right at the other end of the spectrum from relaxation and recovery.

Bringing movement into my meditation wasn't really a conscious decision. What started out as simply dancing to some of my favourite tunes became a sort of lifeline for me and a way of connecting with other people.

I would dance and sometimes I'd share the dance for others to experience it too. I realised that dancing for me was a fast track to my joy, and when we are facing challenges in life we all need something that helps shift things back into perspective.

I would often dance for only one song, but sometimes I would dance for an hour at a time. I was already familiar with ecstatic dance spaces here in the UK, and the sober rave scene was definitely on the rise, but what really inspired me was the introspective internal space that opened up for me through dance.

When I was finally starting to see some shifts in my life, I remember feeling really out of sorts in my then house share in Brixton, south London. I wasn't enjoying being with the people I shared the house with, the environment felt very toxic, and rather than getting up and leaving straight away, as I normally would, I decided to slow things down, closing my eyes and doing some slow movements on my bed, opening up my spine, spiralling, rocking, tapping and doing various Yin Yoga-inspired moves.

Before long a strong wave of emotion came surging through me and I was in floods of tears. I had no idea that I felt so deeply sad until that moment. I knew that the movement had unlocked something for me. It reminded me of my partying days, at a time when I was working through some really heavy grief and somehow being on those sweaty techno dance floors helped me move through a lot of that pain.

I'd found something magic that autumn morning in my room in Brixton, although it wasn't until I moved into my family home for the winter that I was to begin deepening this practice on my own, bringing in all the techniques and training from all my studies in meditation, energy healing, shamanic practices, samba, breath-work, somatic techniques, Yoga, Tai chi and Qigong.

It wasn't until 2022 that I started properly sharing the practice with women, at a small women's community centre in north London called Moon. The feedback was good, although it wasn't until I introduced eye masks that people made big breakthroughs and experienced healing for themselves.

By creating an environment that allows the body to drop into relaxation, we can connect with our true feelings and allow them to pass through. The intention for me was to allow people to enjoy themselves, tapping into their inner child, the part of us that knows how to play unapologetically.

It was as if something had really clicked into place and the more workshops I host, the more I see people leave feeling as if they have had a real breakthrough. One woman danced with her 12-year-old self for two hours, another elderly lady with disabilities said she had to write about it in her book. The reviews and feedback have been profound.

To begin exploring your own sense of movement meditation I encourage you to treat it as an exploration of your body. Although there is a specific method that I teach during my in-person workshops, I don't feel that would translate well on the page, so I have decided to keep it pretty simple, bringing in only a few techniques.

Preparation

To set the scene for your first movement meditation practice, I encourage you to light some incense or a candle, put on some comfortable clothes to move freely in, lay down a yoga mat if you have one, and perhaps grab a bottle of water in case you get thirsty.

If you have an eye mask and feel comfortable wearing one, then I would highly recommend doing so, although it is not essential. If you have a playlist of music ready to go, then great. Otherwise please jump to the end of Chapter Five for a link to one of my past workshop Spotify playlists. It's a 90-minute sonic journey, so there is plenty of material for you to play with. If you are not using my playlist, I recommend you create one with a focus on instrumental music.

Begin by putting on your music.

Now adopt a comfortable seated position, ideally on a yoga mat, with your eyes either closed or covered with an eye mask.

You can start to bring some gentle touch to your body by cupping different parts of the body with your hands. I recommend starting with the feet and working your way up to the top of the head, although you can start at the head and work your way down to your feet. You can choose to gently pat, or squeeze each body part as you go. You can spend anywhere between a few seconds to a minute in each area.

Often with this exercise we realise it has been a while since we have given various body parts any attention, especially the feet, which do so much for us every day. Treat this part as a self-love exercise, bringing your full presence to the practice. Imagine you are stroking a loved one, or perhaps a pet. Bring that much gentleness and care to your touch.

Once you have worked your way around your whole body and with eyes still closed, I'd like you to lie flat on your back, toes facing up to the ceiling and arms outstretched on either side from the body. Begin by starting to rock forward and back from your feet to your head for a few minutes. This sends a signal to your body that you are safe to relax. Safe to let go. Sometimes you might notice little tremors, or yawns, as your heart rate goes down and your parasympathetic nervous system is activated. All these effects are welcome.

After you feel a little more relaxed, come up into child's pose (yoga posture) with your body pushed back towards your heels, head facing down to the mat, and arms outstretched flat on the mat in front of you. You can lie like this for another minute or so before coming up on to your knees and starting to create some gentle movements in a figure of eight, forward and back, always keeping the palms of your hands on the floor, while creating gentle spirals of your spine. This helps to really open the body. Don't forget to breathe throughout, with an elongated exhalation for a count of 8 for maximum effect.

When you are ready, push back into downward dog, and start padding your feet on the floor, creating movement in your legs, opening up the muscles at the back of your legs. Stretch and lengthen your legs before coming up to a standing position.

Now focus on the soles of your feet and start bouncing lightly on your heels with the pads of your feet remaining on the floor. Now start to shake your body, gently at first and more strongly as you go. You want to shake off any heavy energy, whether that be stress from your day or week, or any tension you have been carrying. You can really go for it with your arms, and even add some up-tempo music to this if you feel comfortable doing so.

Once you are all shaken out, I would like you to imagine a golden light is beaming out of your heart and travelling down into the earth below you like a thread, while in the exact opposite direction imagine another beam of golden light travelling up through the crown of your head and into the sky, making a connection from the wider universe down to the core of the earth. Reminding you of your intrinsic connection to nature.

From here you should imagine a beam of light is travelling out from your heart and into the world around you, sending love to the air, the fire, the water and the earth, to the plants, the elements, the crystals and the trees. To the furry ones, four-legged ones, winged ones and creatures of the sky. To all of humanity.

Dancing with your heart or spirit in this way, actively send out loving energy to wherever it is needed. Allow that energy to pour through you and towards you as you dance along to the beat.

Now is your moment to move freely for as long as you like. The music will build in tempo and eventually quieten down, encouraging you to finish in Savasana pose on the floor to fully ground into the earth again before closing the practice.

Some days a couple of songs will do the trick, other days you may want to move for longer.

There isn't a day that goes by where I don't dance. Even in a simple playful way, it helps me get out of my head in the most effective way.

CHAPTER FIVE

Conclusions & Free Guided Meditations

I have always found that with traditional forms of meditation, what works best for me is being in a traditional retreat environment, away from the hustle and bustle of everyday life.

By committing to a 10-day silent retreat, locking my phone away, and having all my meals and meditation schedule prepared by someone else helps to create the perfect environment. It may seem obvious, but meditating at home adds another level of complication. Not only are there other people (family members, house mates, etc) to consider, there are also a whole heap of distractions to navigate, from social media to TV.

And although post-retreat, time and again, my intention was always to return home and continue meditating for a couple of hours a day, it wouldn't be very long before I'd slip into bad habits, finding it nearly impossible to motivate myself to practise every day.

It felt as if the more traditional techniques like Vipassana didn't work well for me in present-day city life. Perhaps some of you may find it easy, but for me it is tough. This led me on a journey to discover the different meditation practises that work for me, exploring techniques that fit into my own lifestyle.

What I have learned is that whatever my mood is on a particular day, any practice or habit that is going to last is ultimately something I have to enjoy. It cannot be something I can easily skip, or postpone because I feel too tired. Or whatever other excuses the mind throws my way.

If am going to stay motivated over time, it has to feel good. If it feels like a chore, or something I 'need' or 'should' be doing, I am quickly off track.

And I am not suggesting all tasks in life are supposed to be easy, I am simply referring to meditation and what has worked for me.

I certainly didn't consciously want meditation to feel like a punishment, yet during my whole 2018 monk-life phase, that definitely became a reality for me. And don't get me wrong, there are literally hundreds of ways to reach enlightenment. And I don't judge any of them.

I have learnt what works through trial and error. For some people, renunciation and moving to a monastery is the way, and for others the path involves living in the thick of civilisation. I am part of the latter crew.

Regardless, and whether you believe in past lives or not, in this life I happen to find myself in one of the biggest cities in the world.

And yes, perhaps in other lifetimes I was on a mountain top, but in this life I find myself working in the corporate world, enjoying the richness of culture and diversity that Western cities like London have to offer, while also navigating the chaos and intensity of it all too.

It took me close to letting go of everything I had to help me realise that there is some enjoyment and value to be found in the material world and entertainment, despite many religions and spiritual teachings warning you against them.

The one big take-out from all this is that you must follow your own path, even if others label it unique, off-beat or alternative.

Dogma can be very confusing. If something feels good and authentic to you, and it is not hurting anyone or causing you or others any harm, but you're told it's inappropriate or wrong, you can end up in a spiritual dilemma.

I recall applying to attend a meditation retreat only for the organisers to reject my application because I was training in energy healing at the time.

It's easy to see how these practices can become quite restrictive, as there is a desire for them to remain pure and intact. However, sometimes it seems restrictive and limiting, given all the flavours, behaviours and colours of humanity at large.

And is that really what the Buddha wanted 2,500 years ago, to create a VIP club only for those who followed the rules, and who ticked this one tiny box?

Whenever I returned from a retreat it wouldn't be long before I began to feel an element of frustration set in. Despite experiencing all the benefits within the bubble of the retreat centre, once I was home it was often straight back to work, with all the daily demands on my time, such as life admin, meal preparation, laundry, cleaning, shopping, fitness, and so on.

London life doesn't leave a lot of free time to dedicate to self-care and meditation. Unless, that is, you want to make some big sacrifices like limiting socialising in the evening, or getting up very early (4am vibes) to fit it all in.

And trust me, I have tried it all, spending most of 2018 living as a monk, relinquishing much of what I used to enjoy for what I deemed was the 'right path', or the noble path as the Buddha would say.

The reality was this approach led to much of my own self-induced suffering. Looking back I can see how I isolated myself, shut out friends, changed my lifestyle habits from one extreme to the other. By rejecting simple pleasures, I was rejecting a part of myself. I hadn't found the middle way that all the teachers speak about; the pendulum had swung too far in the other direction.

I was going through a massive transformation, and some family members and friends couldn't quite grasp what was happening to me. Spirituality can become quite addictive if you're not careful. Anything can become unhealthy if you grasp it too tightly. Ultimately the key to everything is balance, or finding the middle way.

Ironically, it was the pandemic that helped me end that cycle. When the world was locked down, nothing had really changed for me. I was used to spending time alone, I was used to being on retreat, yet what I noticed was how many other people were struggling. With normal life at a standstill, I felt as if there was something I could do to offer support, based on everything I'd learnt.

I started sharing short YouTube video recordings, showing up every day to record guided meditations for people and putting them online.

As I'd recently walked away from a freelance events contract, I had very little paid work at the time, so showing up each day to record a meditation helped keep me grounded. I realised that I had a gift of sharing my voice in this way, and if the meditations helped only one person then it would have been worthwhile.

The daily meditations soon became weekly, and then slowly my energy shifted towards hosting weekly Yoga Nidra calls on Zoom, and soon I was invited to run mindfulness workshops for tech start-ups and small businesses, before eventually running corporate workshops and live meditations to hundreds of people online. I eventually even collaborated on my first in-person retreat.

This book has allowed me to bring together the best bits of everything I have studied and put into practice over the last nine years. I hope you have enjoyed reading it as much as I have enjoyed writing it.

If you would like to stay in touch or practise some other meditations that I have prepared, you can visit these sites online:

Insight Timer: https://insighttimer.com/spiritchild

YouTube: https://www.youtube.com/
@spiritchildofthemoon4555/videos

Spotify Playlist: https://open.spotify.com/playlist/
72eCECeKae6AXEXa5bG4up?si=5dffc02f7afb4d76

Instagram: @gabriellaweekes

Your beginners' guide to the meditation journey is now complete.

I wish you all a wonderful exploration and journey, finding your way with this life-changing supportive practice. Happy meditating.

Love,

Gabriella

Resources

1) Page 8: Josh Howarth, 'Alarming Average Screen Time Statistics', Exploding Topics, Jan 13, 2023
https://explodingtopics.com/blog/screen-time-stats

2) Page 10: Ryan Kane, 'How Many People Meditate In The World?' Mindfulness Box, Sep 6, 2023
https://mindfulnessbox.com/how-many-people-meditate-in-the-world/

3) Page 10: World O Meters, 2023
https://www.worldometers.info/world-population/

4) Page 14: Collins Dictionary
https://www.collinsdictionary.com/dictionary/english/meditation

5) Page 16: Robin Sharma, 'The Monk Who Sold His Ferrari: A Fable About Fulfilling Your Dreams and Reaching Your Destiny', Harpers Thorsons, 2015).

6) Page 26: Corinne Burns, 'Anti-depressant prescribing increases by 35% in six years', Pharmaceutical Journal, July 8, 2022
https://pharmaceutical-journal.com/article/news/antidepressant-prescribing-increases-by-35-in-six-years

7) Page 49: Scott Edwards, 'Dancing and the Brain', Harvard Medical School, Harvard Education, 2015
Dancing and the Brain | Harvard Medical School

8) Page 49: Jamie Ducharme, 'Dance Like Your Doctor Is Watching: It's Great for Your Mind and Body', Time, Dec 20, 2018
Dancing Is Great for Your Mind and Body | Time

About the Author

Gabriella Weekes is a writer, mindfulness expert, dancer, astrologer and event producer originally from London. Her advice on meditation has featured previously in *The Daily Telegraph* newspaper. She has previously written two meditation columns for national magazine titles, *Simply Beautiful Gardens* and *Mindful Crafting,* and published her astrology guide *The Stars Align* in 2021. She has taught meditation to hundreds of people online, while also hosting mindfulness workshops for tech startups, and corporate businesses. Gabriella lives in London with her cat, Cheeks.

would greatly appreciate it if you would write a short review of this book on Amazon, to help me spread the word and share this guide with more people. All you have to do is search this book title on Amazon, and select the customer reviews section. There you will find an option to review this product to write a customer review. Many thanks.

Printed in Poland
by Amazon Fulfillment
Poland Sp. z o.o., Wrocław

22268821R00040